A Guide for the Bereaved Survivor

A List of Reactions, Suggestions, and
Steps for Coping with Grief

Bob Baugher, Ph.D.

About the Author

Dr. Bob Baugher is an instructor at Highline Community College and has been teaching courses in Psychology and Death Education for more than 30 years. As a Fellow in Thanatology through the Association for Death Education and Counseling, Bob has lectured on numerous topics in the field of dying, death, and grief and has given more than 600 workshops. He is a LivingWorks instructor having trained more than1,000 people in suicide intervention. As a counselor and researcher he has worked with bereaved parents and siblings, children and adults who have lost a parent, widows and widowers, cancer patients, and brain-injured individuals and their families. At the 2001 national conference of The Compassionate Friends, Bob received the Professional of the Year award for his supportive work with bereaved parents and siblings.

Having experienced the loss of a loved one through a sudden death, Marc Calija took Bob's course in Death Education. He suggested to Bob the idea for the original book. As a result, Bob and Marc co-authored the original version of this book titled, *A Guide for the Bereaved Survivor Who Has Lost a Loved One through a Sudden Death*.

Dedication

This book is dedicated to the memory of:

Joel Melville whose 1978 death by murder inspired the original version of this book.

de Olsen, co-founder of the Seattle chapter of The Compassionate Friends (TCF)

Vic Ellison, TCF chapter leader and Parents of Murdered Children chapter member

Mother, Eleanor Baugher and Father, Bob Baugher, Sr.

Father-in-law, Chief Brown and Mother-in-law, Millie Brown

Brother-in-law, Jeff Keller

Table of Contents

Introduction

Some Comments Before You Read This Book

Someone you love has died. While your love will never fade, this book may be one of the ways to help you begin the long and painful road of working on your grief. Maybe you have read or heard that there are specific feelings you have to go through; but that is not necessarily true. If you are reading this to support someone, it is important to allow any feelings that come up.

While you may experience some of the listed grief reactions and may benefit from some of the suggestions, not all may apply to you. The lists of reactions in this book are meant to be brief in order to provide you with an overview of the bereavement process. The reactions do not occur in any particular order (although shock and denial tend to occur first). You may see some reactions recycle as time goes by. In a matter of seconds you can find yourself going from having a pleasant moment to experiencing several grief reactions at once. The listed reactions do not describe any one person; but from the lists you can identify some of what you are going through.

The suggestions are based upon research findings and from the experiences of people who have suffered losses such as the death of a child, sibling, spouse, partner, parent, other relative, or friend. Choose the suggestions that will help you as each of us grieves differently and within our own time. No one can rush you through this.

Research on bereaved individuals has shown that people who are thrust into a painful situation may not be fully aware of the effects of such a devastating event. Although reading this book may not take away the hurt, my hope is that it can tell you something about the pain of your loss. People who have read this book have reported that, as they coped with their grief, they picked up the book at various times over the weeks, months, and years to compare their earlier responses to their later ones.

One way of looking at the bereavement process is called the Two-Track Model [1].* What this means is the death of a loved one involves two major reactions:

1. Grief process that includes emotions, thoughts, physical responses, and social issues

*Throughout the book you will see numbers in brackets [ ]. These represent research articles or books that can be found in the Reference section on page 77.

2. Our ongoing relationship with the person who died [2, 3]. This means new ways of relating to and remembering the deceased person.

This book will focus on the grief process (#1), but will also examine the bond you may still feel with the person who died.

To Keep in Mind as You Read This Book

- Due to the loss, your concentration level may be temporarily affected and reading may be difficult for you.

- Beginning on page 2, this book has been formatted so that you will find one grief reaction on the even numbered pages and a set of suggestions for coping on the odd numbered pages.

- If you find that you can only read two or three pages at a time, put the book down and come back to it later. In addition, you can jump to any relevant page in an instant.

- This book contains a variety of suggestions. They come from scientific research studies of thousands of bereaved people as well as from personal suggestions from the people who contributed to the book.

- Some of the reactions or suggestions are repeated in more than one section of this book. Grief, in all of its complexity, requires that we revisit some of the issues.

- One of the goals of this book is to keep it brief, yet informative. If you are interested in a deeper understanding of particular issues, you can visit the website www.centering.org to order any of hundreds of books on grief. In addition, the website for the Association for Death Education and Counseling provides many resources on coping with grief and loss: www.adec.org.

- Although grief does not arrive in orderly categories, this book has been divided into four main sections to help you begin to sort out the confusing world of grief:

    Emotional Reactions

    Physical Reactions

    Reactions to Others

    Thought-Related Reactions

Let's look first at Emotional Reactions.

Emotional Reactions

SHOCK

- You may feel stunned, dazed, overwhelmed when you are first informed of the death.

- It is clear that shock is a common reaction to a sudden death. However, even if the death was due to a terminal illness, you may still find yourself in shock.

- If you viewed the body, similar feelings may emerge.

- Statements such as these can indicate shock:
  "My head feels numb."
  "What's wrong with me?"
  "I don't feel anything."
  "I'm so confused. I can't think straight."
  "The world is spinning around me."

- Some people report that the whole incident can later seem like a dream or like a movie repeating itself over and over in their minds.

- Other responses may include:
  Shortness of breath
  Screaming
  Problems in speaking
  Being unable to cry
  Being unable to stop crying
  Numbness
  Confusion

- Many people report feeling like a robot as they went through the motions of daily living and watching the world go on as if nothing had happened.

- Similarly, other people talk about being on "automatic pilot;" and they were later amazed that they were able to accomplish anything during this stressful time. Yet, they did.

Suggestions

Shock is a **natural** response to a crisis. Because your mind is reacting to an explosion of new information, shock is the brain's way of insulating you against the full impact of the loss. As time goes on, you will begin to see evidence of the shock wearing off as other emotions begin to emerge.

Because being in shock can interfere with your ability to make sound decisions, most experts on grief suggest waiting to make decisions to give away or sell any of the deceased person's belongings. It is okay to keep items now and decide later. More about this on page 63.

Long after a loss, many people look back on the first weeks and months following the death and realize that they had been in some degree of shock. As the shock wore off, they began to feel more of the raw emotions of their loss. This is one of the main reasons why, months after a death, bereaved people often report feeling worse. Therefore, as your numbness subsides, you will more than likely begin to experience more fully some of the other grief reactions noted in this book.

The information in the next paragraph is for people who have just found out that their loved one has died:

Before you see the body, ask the person in charge to give you some idea of what you will see. Understand that the death process will immediately begin to change the way the person looks. Be sure to bring a support person with you.

If you want to know about the condition of your loved one's body, manner of death, or evidence of injury, do not hesitate to ask questions. Do not let the reactions of others discourage you. You have a right to know.

Consider making an appointment later with a contact person in the Medical Examiner's Office (coroner), the police department, or the hospital. This is something you can do months, even years later in order to get your questions answered.

HYPERACTIVITY

- Upon hearing the news of the death or viewing the body, some people have reported falling to their knees or falling to the floor.

- You may experience a heightened need to move around.

- Your body may have the sudden sensation of being intensely stimulated.

- You may experience a feeling of dizziness or light-headedness.

- You may have a need to sigh, that is, to inhale and try to catch your breath. For some people this reaction can continue for months.

- Well-meaning people may tell you to relax, sit down, or stay put.

- Many people describe feeling like a trapped animal.

- Periods of disorientation may come and go in which events may seem to be happening so rapidly that it is difficult to make sense of incoming information.

- Your brain may feel like it is going to explode. You may feel a need to scream, moan, cry loudly and/or wail; or your shock may be so great you have none of these reactions.

- Problems may seem overwhelming.

- Some people report feeling like they were having a panic attack.

- You may say to yourself, "I've got to take care of all these problems but I can't even take care of myself right now."

Suggestions

People make it through these reactions even though at the time it feels like they won't.

Upon hearing the news of the death or viewing the body, find a safe area where you can move about without risking harm to yourself or interfering with others.

If you decide to go some place, recognize that your thinking processes, reaction time, and coordination may not be up to par.

Consider letting someone else do the driving for you during this time.

To help with your need for sighing, take a *deep* breath and hold it for a few seconds. Then continue to breathe normally. Do this whenever you say, "I can't breathe." or "I can't catch my breath."

Especially during times of hyperactivity, finding someone who can help you focus on one problem at a time can help with some of your disorientation. Ask yourself, "Who is the best available person?" Then contact that person and directly state, "I need you to be with me."

You may want to ask this person to hug you or simply hold your hand.

It doesn't matter how long it has been since the death: It is okay to ask for help. You deserve it. In most cases people will want to help you. So, ask and ask again until you get the help you need.

DENIAL

- Denial is a refusal or inability to admit a truth.

- Because your brain holds thousands of memories of this person still alive, you will find yourself in denial. Your brain may be processing the harsh and unforgiving fact of the death over and over and over (and over) again because this new information is so foreign to you.

- It is common to think:

  "No! This is not happening!"
  "It can't be true!"
  "What this person is saying is wrong!"
  "No way."
  "It's like a nightmare—a bad dream."
  "I can't believe it."
  "This is unreal."

- You may find yourself expecting this person to be in another part of your house or to come walking through the door any minute. You might expect a message or a call. These expectations may come and go for months—maybe longer.

- It can be helpful to think of the denial process on a scale that ranges from 100% denial, which is total *non-recognition* of the reality of the death to 0% denial, which is total *recognition* of the reality of the death:

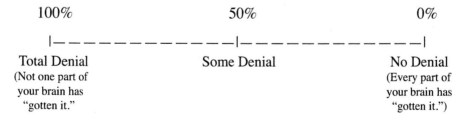

- Answer the following question, "Where am I on the above scale at this moment?"

- As denial and shock begin to wear off, other grief reactions, such as anger and sadness, may begin to emerge. However, as these other reactions come to light, you may find yourself moving back into denial, even just for a few seconds. Expect this recycling of denial to continue for months and years.

Suggestions

Denial is normal. Most experts agree that during the early periods of grief it is *impossible* for the human mind to grasp the full reality of the death because, as stated before, our brain has thousands of cells loaded with memories of this person alive and well. In other words, your grieving brain cannot "get" it.

One of the most critical tasks of grief work is to confront and experience the reminders that the loss has occurred at a level you can tolerate [4]. For example, some people will flood themselves with reminders such as looking at pictures and listening to songs soon after the death. Other people cannot bring themselves to do this until sometime later. See page 16 for discussion of reminders. Confronting the reminders can be painful; but the alternative is to avoid them at the expense of staying at the higher end of the Denial Scale.

While you may at times want to talk about the deceased person, other people in your life may want to avoid such discussions altogether. They may feel this silence is less painful for you—and for them. If appropriate, tell them that talking about this person is not only OK, it is desired. You can tell people you just want them to listen while you talk about your loved one; or they can add their stories as well.

Some bereaved people find it is helpful to talk about their thoughts and feelings, while others seem to cope just fine by keeping them inside [5].

Find someone who listens. Suggestions for being a good listener can be found on page 45.

Months or years later something might happen and you may find yourself saying, "It is impossible that he's gone. I just can't believe it." This is normal.

As difficult as it might be, try to consider it a normal progression in your grief process when you begin to experience less denial and more of the other grief reactions listed in this book.

EMOTIONAL NUMBNESS

- Not feeling at all or very little is numbness. Emotional numbness in relation to the death could last a few moments to several hours, days, or longer.

- When asked, "How do you feel?" you may experience an absence of emotional feeling and say, "I don't feel anything." Emotional numbness could mark the beginning stages of shock and denial. Friends and family may incorrectly interpret your lack of reaction as evidence that you are somehow already beginning to "adjust" to the death.

- You may be unable to cry.

- Early in the bereavement process (especially if it was a sudden death), emotional numbness could mask other feelings such as sadness and anger.

- Emotional numbness can be troubling to people who believe they should be reacting to the death. For example, some people report that at first they felt no guilt or anger only to see it emerge later. Emotional numbness can involuntarily postpone a range of emotions during the early period of grief.

- During the period of numbness, people may incorrectly believe that they have somehow avoided the more difficult and painful aspects of the bereavement process. Weeks and months later, as the numbness begins to wear off, they are surprised when other grief reactions appear. A common statement is, "I feel worse now than I did weeks [or months] ago."

- You also may have feelings that you are reluctant to share and may respond, "I'm fine." or "I'm okay." because you choose not to admit to yourself and/or others how you feel.

- As time goes by, you may find that this numbness evolves to feelings of emptiness. Many bereaved people report walking around feeling empty inside during the months following the death.

- The world may look "different."

- You may wonder why the world is continuing to function as if nothing has happened.

Suggestions

The reactions of shock, denial, body numbness, and emotional numbness all work together to protect you from the incredible overload that would take place in your mind, body, and spirit if you received the full impact of your loss all at once. While these naturally protective reactions may be confusing to you and to other people in your life, your brain's natural tendency is to defend itself from pain by insulating and numbing itself.

As you begin to feel the reality of the death sink in, it may be helpful to say to yourself, "My brain is beginning to 'get' it — the numbness is wearing off."

This "wearing off" of the numbness will continue for months. For many people this diminishing numbness ushers in more pain. It's similar to what happens when your body is first injured: You may feel numb at first, but after a time, your body begins to feel again.

If you have chosen to share your feelings of grief, you may have discovered that people respond to you in a variety of ways. For example, they may not understand how you feel because your grief process is constantly changing and even you may be having a hard time understanding what you are going through. Moreover, in the case of close family members and friends, they may be experiencing their own array of grief reactions.

Some people will seem to ignore how you feel.

At other times they will listen intently.

Yet, sometimes people will appear to not be in a caring mood.

Consider taking the risk to be honest with your feelings. Keep looking for *safe* opportunities to be heard. Find someone who can listen to your grief without judgment. You might begin the conversation by stating that your grief reactions may not only be hard to share, but hard to hear. Sharing your feelings is important, especially as the numbness begins to wear off.

Many bereaved people find comfort in talking to people who have had a similar loss. When they hear other's stories of loss, they begin to realize their emptiness will not last forever. Support groups for the type of loss you are experiencing can be found on the Internet.

In order to gain some perspective on grief, some bereaved people begin to keep a diary. In it you can note any changes as time passes. An alternative to writing is using a voice recorder to talk about your grief. People who used these methods reported that, when they revisited their words months and years later, it gave them a sense of perspective, that is, "Here's where I was compared to where I am now."

DEEP SADNESS AND DEPRESSION

- In describing this aspect of grief, some experts prefer the term *deep sadness* rather than depression. Depression differs from sadness in that it is a combination of sadness **and** pessimism. Depression will lead a person to believe that things will *never* get better.

- One of the main differences between sadness due to loss and other types of sadness or depression is the following: if the loss were to be reversed—for example if by some miracle the deceased person were able to come back—the sadness would vanish.

- Words that have been used to describe these feelings are:

Agony	Hell upon earth	Suffering
Desolation	Hopeless	Tortured
Despair	Lousy	Lonely
Despondent	Miserable	Unhappy
Discouragement	Painful	
Heartache	Sorrowful	

- You may want to cry, sob, weep, or wail. You might cry so hard you cannot breathe. You may hurt so bad that you wonder if you could survive this heartbreak.

- The sadness you feel from the death is due largely to countless additional losses: the person's presence, personality, touch, comfort, companionship, and future to name a few. In addition, you feel the loss of caring for someone you love. You may have lost the person who considered you number 1.

- You may feel sad when you think of how your loved one fought so hard to live.

- Your sadness may also come from watching the effect of the death on your family members.

- Sadness can be experienced in the form of *grief attacks* in which you suddenly become upset and/or begin crying. You may be surprised at your reaction. A grief attack can be caused by reminders that trigger emotions. Grief attacks can be upsetting because the trigger that brought on the reaction is not always apparent. For example, if you walked into a room today that has a slight hint of the scent of the hospital room where your loved one died, you might suddenly begin to feel upset, even if you are unaware of the reason.

Suggestions

Sadness and depression are normal reactions to loss. One woman described her loss as follows: "It felt like a tree in my heart had been ripped out by the roots."

It is okay to feel lousy. Some days will be worse than others. There is no logical progression to these feelings.

Cry and cry if you need to. Don't listen to well-meaning friends who tell you not to cry.

To repeat: Do not suppress crying. It is a natural channel through which your mind and body can work through the pain.

Some people cry a great deal, some cry a little, and some don't cry at all. Whatever you do is okay. If you are not a crier or haven't cried, don't be hard on yourself. Some people do not cry following a death and they do just fine. If people in your life are not crying over the death, let them be. While crying can be helpful to some, it is not a requirement to effectively cope with a loss.

Are you concerned about crying "too much?" Most experts in this area feel that there is no such thing as crying too much. A poem says it best:
> *Today I'll cry*
> *Until I'm dry*
> *Tears held back today*
> *May leave tomorrow with more to pay*

Some people derive comfort by having a "talk" with the person who died. Many people report continuing to do so for years. It only becomes unhealthy when the bereaved person denies the reality of the death.

Writing a letter to the person who died can be another way to cope with grief. Contents can include: events that have occurred since the death, memories of the life lived, and things you didn't get a chance to say. This is not a good-bye letter. The act of writing can be a way to work on some unfinished business and still feel some connection to this person. Perhaps there were conflicts or ill feelings that never got resolved. Many people find this type of writing a healthy way to cope.

When you find yourself in the middle of a grief attack, find a way to try to soothe yourself (if at all possible) by saying, "These terrible feelings are upsetting me right now, but they will eventually subside."

Dealing with your sadness, grief attacks, and pessimism—the belief that things will never get better—will take time. Talking to people who have similar experiences, such as people in a support group, can help. Most people report that the intensity of these reactions gradually lessens, but that some of these feelings never entirely go away.

GUILT

- Guilt is remorseful awareness stemming from a perception of having done something wrong or failing to have done something. Guilt feelings can be very powerful as they have a way of convincing us of our offenses whether or not we had anything to do with the death.

- Common feelings of guilt can stem from [6]:
  Words said or not said
  Feeling like you didn't do enough to relieve your loved one's suffering
  Not reacting to what now seemed to be a "premonition"
  Feelings about not living up to expectations
  Medical care decisions
  Surviving
  Not spending enough time with this person
  Not being present when the moment of death occurred
  Unresolved issues with this person
  Something you did related to the cause of the death
  Something you didn't do related to the cause of the death
  Engaging in sexual relations
  Not grieving enough
  Grieving "too much"
  Feeling like you are forgetting the person
  Not doing enough when your loved one needed help
  Being involved in a new relationship
  Feeling like you failed in your role
  Feeling better
  Having other emotional reactions to the loss, such as anger or envy toward others
  Feeling like you are moving on
  Enjoying life

- The guilt you feel may be from the relief that the problems associated with the life of this person one will no longer exist.

- Examples of guilt statements

  "I feel guilty (or responsible)"   "I don't deserve to. . . ."
  "If only. . . ."   "It's my fault."
  "Why didn't I. . . ."   "It should've been me."
  "I should have. . . ."   "I shouldn't have. . . ."

- Friends and family may say, "You shouldn't feel guilty."

Suggestions

Guilt is one of the most common reactions to a death. If you are feeling any degree of guilt, you have joined a very large group. Go ahead and feel guilty, but consider some of the suggestions that follow.

Whatever you were doing when the death occurred, you were doing what you felt was the right thing to do at the time. Now, looking back, it is easy to say, "I should have done it another way." The term *Hindsight Bias* [7] refers to our tendency to look back on an event and say, "I should have seen this coming." Or "I should have done something about this." Watch yourself when you use the word *should*. You can **never go back and reverse a** *should have*. You can only do something now.

Performing a ritual may help. Light a "guilt candle," say what you need to say and blow it out. Find a pebble or rock and designate it your "guilt rock." Over time gradually relocate it from your room to outside your home until you are ready to throw it away along with your guilt.

If you plan to see the body, say aloud or in your mind all the things to this person that you didn't get a chance to say before.

Venture to a place where you feel closest to that person and express your guilt. Some people choose the cemetery—others choose a special place. Many people find this a helpful way to ease some of the guilt over not saying what needed to be said while the person was alive.

As noted earlier, many people find it helpful to write a letter saying things that had been left unsaid, such as "I'm sorry . . . ." or "I love you."

Feeling guilty is natural. To better manage your guilt, ask yourself:
 Who is a good listener who can hear me talk about my guilt feelings?
 How long am I going to continue to "beat myself up"?
 What would it take for me to begin to forgive myself?
 Would my loved one want me to be feeling like this?
 What if my loved one were to suddenly appear before me for ten seconds and say
  something about all the guilt I've been feeling? What words would I hear? (Some people
  report hearing or feeling that they heard comforting words from their loved one.)

Do you somehow feel controlled from the grave? Does your guilt stem from feelings that you somehow are not (or were not) living up to the expectations of the deceased person? If so, you may want to find a good listener who can help you work on this.

Take the energy that you have given to guilt and channel it into a project. Many people do volunteer work or create something new in the name of the person who died.

SELF-PUNISHMENT

- Some people engage in dangerous behaviors:
    Excessive drinking or drug use
    Inflicting physical pain on one's body
    Not giving appropriate medical attention to an injury, wound, or possible illness
    Driving recklessly
    Engaging in risk-taking behavior without regard to consequences ("If I get hurt or die, so what?")

- Consciously or unconsciously you may omit or neglect your everyday needs:
    Eating
    Sleeping
    Permitting yourself daily comforts
    Communicating with other people
    Being good to yourself

- You may believe that you do not "deserve" to do pleasurable things such as:
    Laughing
    Going out to a movie, sports event, dinner
    Giving or receiving affection
    Engaging in sexual behavior
    Vacationing
    Participating in other recreational activities

- Apathy as another form of self-punishment can best be described as "not caring for life." It can stem from emotional numbness or deep sadness and presents as lack of energy. Common statements include:
    "Why go on? What's the use?"
    "I'm not afraid of dying."
    "I just don't care about things anymore."
    "Why do anything when life doesn't have meaning?"
These statements reflect normal feelings of grief. It may sound surprising to hear that it is okay to feel lousy and to have these negative thoughts. You are experiencing the grief of a profound loss and your suffering mind is doing the best that it can under the circumstances.

Suggestions

Recognizing excessive and unhealthy forms of self-punishment is a critical step to managing your grief.

As much as you may not feel like it, do all you can to eliminate self-punishing behaviors. You may feel, as do some bereaved people, that somehow the death of this person is "proof" that you are a bad person or that there is a "curse" on you or your family. Even though this may *seem* true, it is critical that you come to understand that **the death does not define who you are**.

Don't hurt yourself. If your thoughts of self-harm continue, tell someone and get the help you need. Your loved one would want you to be taking care of yourself and to be good to yourself, especially at a time like this.

Some bereaved people think seriously about suicide for a time after the death. Ask yourself the following question: "Would I want to add another death to my family's already overwhelming grief?"

Eating a balanced diet and getting sufficient sleep will enable you to cope more effectively with the other grief reactions you are having to your loss. If you take a sleep aide, consult with your doctor.

Do you have thoughts of "What's the use?" Be patient with yourself. As terrible as you feel right now, please understand the following will be true for you:

At some point in the future you will not feel this awful.

It may seem impossible right now, but millions of people have felt some of your feelings and absolutely believed that they would always feel that way only to later discover that they did feel better. Not back to normal—but better than they ever believed they could at the time.

REMINDERS

- Your precious loved one died too soon. For most people one of the most painful aspects of death is missing the person. The constant absence is hard to endure [8].

- It will seem that everywhere you look, memories of a life lived are triggered. Some are painful, some bring a smile, and some will surprise you.

  Examples are:
  Anniversaries, birthdays, holidays, celebrations
  Another death
  Certain people
  Clothing
  Dreams
  Items that come in the mail or on the Internet
  A person with the same first name
  Pictures, movies
  Smells, foods
  Songs
  Sounds
  Special places
  Sports events, school events, graduation, plays
  Words & phrases

- The holiday season, with its sights, sounds, and smells in the air may bring tears as precious memories are triggered.

- You may even cry at seemingly insignificant situations.

- During the weeks leading up to the date of the death many people report increased grief reactions.

- Some people report being shocked at first when they answer the phone and the caller's voice sounds like their deceased loved one. This can "take your breath away."

- Behavior in which you find yourself looking for the person is a common occurrence. Long after the death, when people are asked, "Does your heart still skip a beat when you see someone who looks like the person who died?" their answer is a resounding, "Yes!"

Suggestions

Your mind has a multitude of memories of this precious person that will be stimulated by incidents in the course of your daily activities. You will find some memories comforting, some neutral, and some very painful. However, as each painful memory is confronted again and again, the intensity of the grief reaction tends to diminish.

In the early part of the grief process some of the reminders will feel overwhelming.

Because of the intense pain associated with death, there is a natural tendency to cope by distracting yourself. This is normal. It is your mind's way of protecting itself from additional pain. An effective way to cope with grief is to *balance* this natural protective response with the necessary and healthy confrontation of reminders.

Another way to think about the balancing process is in the form of a natural grief reaction known as the Dual-Process Model of Coping [9]. Many times a day we find ourselves moving back and forth between loss-orientation (feeling the pain) and restoration-orientation (living life without our loved one). For example, as a man is filling out forms from the hospital where his mother died (restoration-orientation) he may suddenly feel tears well up (loss-orientation) as all the emotions of her illness and death come flooding back.

Although confronting painful reminders is difficult, doing so can be a constructive coping mechanism. For example, a woman whose husband died last year decided to drive to the ocean to the exact spot they sat on the beach. The first time she did this she cried the entire time. By the fifth visit her tears had subsided and she was able to feel more positive about the visit.

Conversely, the continued avoidance of places, situations, and people may inhibit the reduction of grief's intensity. However, decide when the time is right for you to confront a painful reminder. Comfort yourself with positive memories.

The searching behavior mentioned earlier continues for many people for a long period of time. Months, even years after the death you may catch yourself thinking, "I've got to tell him about that."

As time goes by, you may begin to see some of the reminders as a positive way of telling you that your loved one has lived a life and, though physically absent, this special person continues to exist in your memory and the memory of others.

ANGER

- Anger is a natural response to being deprived of something valued [10].

- Although many grieving people do feel anger, others may not. It is important to understand that you do not have to feel anger during bereavement.

- Anger can be a reaction to specific situations or people. Alternatively, feelings of anger can be generalized.

- A certain incident may trigger anger that is out of proportion to the situation. Some of your anger may be misdirected at someone as a scapegoat or substitute for what you are actually angry about.

- Targets for anger can include:

The person responsible for the death	Anyone associated with the death
Friends	Life in general
Relatives	The person who died
Coworkers	Yourself
God	Strangers

- Other target groups include:

Health care professionals	Police and detectives
Medical examiner or coroner	Therapists
Funeral home director	People who aren't supportive
People who blame you or the person who died for the death	

- Are you angry for any of the following reasons?
   The needless suffering that your loved one went through
   Upset at the significant life changes produced by the death
   Frustration at other people who don't (or can't) understand
   Difficulty with people who still have their loved ones, but don't
      realize how lucky they are
   Upset at oneself for real or imagined mistakes associated with the death
   A way to regain some lost power and helplessness brought about by the death
   Jealous at what other people have

Suggestions

It is natural to feel anger. Yet, how you express and cope with your anger is important.

Identify your anger issues by answering these questions:
> With whom am I upset regarding this death?
> What are the reasons for my anger?
> What are the triggers for my anger?
> What can I do about my anger?
> Have I been scapegoating innocent parties?
> Is there a way to channel my anger into something positive?

People may not understand your anger. If you are willing, tell them about your anger; but do so at a time when you are not feeling so angry. Try to express your feelings with *I-messages* ("I feel bothered by what you said.") instead of *You-messages* ("You make me so angry.")

It is common to feel anger toward anyone who you perceive as having mistreated you or the person who died. Also common is anger toward anyone you see as guilty for the death, including yourself. If there is an unknown offender, you may experience some generalized anger, a feeling of helplessness, or fear for your own life.

If you are experiencing bodily sensations that require a release, then using safe means to do so is a healthy way of coping. Some suggestions are:
> As soon as you feel the anger begin to increase, count to 10 and take a break before you do or say something you'll later regret.
> Take a brisk walk or other form of exercise
> Find someone to give you a massage

Find someone you can talk with about your anger in particular and your grief reactions in general. Support groups can be a very helpful way to address these issues.

Three important stipulations for expressing anger are:
1. Do **not** hurt other people.
2. Do **not** hurt yourself.
3. Anger is a problem when it takes over your life. If you frequently raise your voice, destroy property, get upset easily, experience road rage, or are in a constant state of general anger, please seek professional help.

Hurting yourself or others means your anger is out of control. Make an appointment now.

FEAR

- Death brings out all of our worst fears, such as fear of:
    Abandonment or being alone
    Breaking down in front of other people at inappropriate times
    Getting the same disease or dying in a similar manner
    Losing your mind
    Forgetting the details of this person's life
    Forgetting the lessons learned from the death
    Getting too busy with life and forgetting at times to sufficiently mourn
    Losing the memory of how this person sounded, felt, smelled
    Not remembering to perform an act or ritual
    Other people forgetting the life of your loved one
    Getting rid of personal effects
    Going out into the world
    Feeling this way for the rest of your life
    Life in general
    The incredible, permanent changes that have taken place in your life
    Losing friends who cannot handle your grief
    The feeling that your loved one did not make it into heaven
    Losing other relatives and friends through death
    Talking with others about the death because of a pending lawsuit
    Loving someone that much again
    Not being able to survive the intense pain of bereavement
    Other terrible things happening in your life
    Spirits, ghosts, or any aspects of the afterlife
    The belief that the death was punishment by God
    What people will say about you or the person who died, especially if the death
        was due to a stigmatized cause, such as AIDS, suicide, homicide, drug-
        or alcohol-related
    The future

Now, go through the list and put a check mark next to those fears that apply to you at this time. Then, circle the fears you can do something about.

Suggestions

It is okay to be afraid at this time in your life. Fear reactions can help us to avoid further pain, although excessive fear can paralyze us.

Look again at the marks you made on the previous page and answer the following:

Can I more clearly define these fears?

With whom should I speak regarding each fear?

What can I do to reduce each fear? Can I make a list?

Can I let go of the fears over which I have no control?

If I cannot let go, what is the worst thing that could happen?

How likely is it that this will happen?

Are there fears that are significantly disrupting my life? If so, should I seek

counseling to begin work on them?

Find people whom you feel can understand you and take the risk to tell them about your fears. Joining a support group can help with this because you can see that other people have similar fears and you can learn new ways of coping.

One of the main fears of bereaved people is forgetting some of the details of their loved one's life and worrying that other people will do the same. If this applies to you, then here are suggestions from people who did something about their fear:

Tell people that you want to hear stories of your loved one.

Put photographs on a video accompanied by music.

Make an audio recording of this person's voice from phone messages.

Make a quilt for your bed from this person's clothing.

Put an ornament on a tree with a picture of your loved one.

For more suggestions see page 23.

ANXIETY OVER FADING MEMORIES

- One of the most anxiety-producing features of death is forgetting the life that was lived. We fear that, with the inevitable passage of time, the memories of our loved one will be lost like tiny drops in the ocean of thousands of memories.

- As the weeks and months turn to years our lives have become bombarded with new experiences and numerous distractions. Events and people have moved in and out of our life. And, as a result, our loved one seems to be moving further from our grasp.

- Another source of anxiety is related to the belief that letting go of the pain of our grief means letting go of the memories and connection with the person who died. It is considered one of *the cruelest tricks of grief*, and it goes something like this:

   Because our reaction to death brings intense pain, which in turn causes grief, this pain becomes integrated within the brain cells of the previously pleasant memories of this person's life. Later, whenever we even think about this person, these previously comforting thoughts may now bring pain and grief. Here is a sketch of the process:

   death → pain → grief → memories → pain → grief

- Furthermore, for many bereaved people, as grief begins to slowly subside, the memories of the life of this person may also begin to appear to slip further into the distance. When this happens, it can create a panic reaction—a feeling of losing our grasp of our loved one. To combat this, we seek ways to hold tight to this person, which—because our memories are now tied to pain—includes holding tight to grief.

- What we all know about grief is the following fact: with time, the pain softens even though at the moment it doesn't feel like it ever will. For many of us, the pain and ensuing grief may never totally disappear. However, our challenge as a bereaved person is to find ways to permit the lessening of the pain of grief while continuing to hold the memories of the person who died.

Suggestions

You know this fact: *You will never forget your loved one.* Many people put their hand on their chest and say, "I hold my loved one here, in my heart."

Memories can be preserved in a number of ways:
  Create a picture album or a slide show.
  Find videos of this person's life—don't forget to ask friends and relatives.
  Write memories in a story form. Some people have written a book.
  Create a memorial website.
  Visit special places. As noted earlier, the first visits may produce sadness.
  Wear the clothing or jewelry of this person.
  Use their items or carry an item with you.
  Make a pillow with this person's picture and/or name (hug it).
  Do things your loved one liked to do.
  Every visit to the beach write their name in the sand and take a picture—
    ask other people to do the same.
  Get a tattoo.
  Plant something or create a memorial garden.
  Light a candle on special occasions.
  Put pictures in places of your choice. Do not let well-meaning people tell you,
    "Isn't it about time to take down this picture?" It is your loss and your decision
    After some time, some people decide themselves to take down a picture—
    but all in their own good time—if ever.
Some people have donated in the following ways:
  Given to a charity
  Participated in a fund-raising event
  Created a scholarship
  Volunteered

Consider the following ways of compiling stories by asking others:
  1. To share their stories in writing.
  2. To meet with you. Bring a voice recorder or video recorder.
  3. To visit a memorial website to leave messages and post stories.
Do not delay working on this project because you are not guaranteed that any of these people will be alive another day. With their death you will have lost some wonderful stories. See page 41 for suggestions on ways to stimulate the memories of these potential contributors.

A Look into Some Physical Reactions

(Remember, some or all of the following reactions may occur. All are normal reactions to loss and, as time goes on, they will decrease or disappear.)

BODY NUMBNESS

- While emotional numbness is more a lack of emotional feeling, body numbness is experienced as diminished physical sensations.

- You may feel light-headed.

- You may feel as if your body "isn't there."

- You may feel like you're on automatic pilot.

- When people ask how you feel, you might reply, "Numb. . . I don't feel much of anything."

- You may find that you frequently repeat yourself.

- Your reaction times may be compromised and you may find yourself responding more slowly to people and situations you encounter.

- The world may seem to be moving in slow motion.

- You may be more sensitive to noises and/or to light.

- Your stomach may be upset.

- The food you eat may taste dull.

Suggestions

Though not everyone experiences body numbness, this state may last only a few hours or as long as several months.

As time goes on you will begin to notice yourself coming out of the fog.

Because you may not be as much in touch with your body during this time, make sure that you are drinking enough water and eating food that is good for you.

Making an appointment for a physical exam can help expose physical problems that are sometimes masked by a myriad of grief reactions.

As both the emotional and physical numbness begin to wear off, you may begin to experience other grief reactions such as pain, sadness, and anger. While these reactions are unpleasant, they are indications that you are beginning to move beyond your numbness and proceed with the painful, but necessary progression into grief.

CHANGES IN EATING AND DRINKING HABITS

- Experiencing grief can alter habits such as eating, cooking, alcohol use, sleeping and pill-taking.

- People often lose their desire to shop for food, cook meals, and eat resulting in inconsistent eating patterns.

- Grabbing the first thing available (often lacking in nutritional value) is a common occurrence.

- Be mindful of grief-induced weight-loss in which a person falls into the trap of believing that this is a positive method for shedding pounds. The reinforcement becomes stronger as the pounds come off and appetite loss is not seen as negative. This can be dangerous because of the lack of vitamins and minerals that can ensue.

- For some people, food becomes a source of comfort, and overeating becomes a problem. Weight gain can become an added burden to the already overwhelming array of grief reactions.

- Has there been an increase in alcohol use since the death? People who had alcohol problems prior to the death usually continue to have such problems. For others, alcohol seems to provide both a way to numb the pain and a way to "forget." If drinking has increased, please seek help.

- Do you use prescribed or over-the-counter medications to manage your grief? Consult with your physician if you have been altering the prescribed dosage or have begun trying new medication combinations.

Suggestions

Changes in eating and drinking can be ways that people attempt to cope with the pain of grief. In moderation the changes can be considered within the range of reasonable coping behaviors. However, when the changes begin to disrupt your life-style, such as your ability to handle the details of daily living, it is important to bring those behaviors under control. If you are unable to do so, professional help may be needed.

Watch for a significant weight loss or gain. Call your doctor if this is beginning to happen.

Even though you may not feel like grocery shopping, find a way to do so and make sure you buy foods from the fruit and vegetable section. Purchase nutritious foods. Freeze leftovers.

Avoid large packages of junk foods. If you wish to treat yourself to sweets, go ahead and do so, but buy small packages. For example, don't buy the two-pound bag of M & M's or a dozen donuts. Instead buy a few at a time, individually wrapped.

Avoid the alcohol aisle altogether. If you must buy alcohol, purchase it in limited quantities, such as a 6-pack of beer or small containers of wine.

Well-meaning people may offer you alcohol because they feel it could help you to relax or to "forget" for a time. You need to be able to say, "No thank you."

As a depressant alcohol lowers inhibitions. Do not put yourself in a situation in which your altered state can make you an easy target for involvement in sexual situations that you may later regret. Widowed persons may be especially vulnerable to such involvement.

Although you may not feel like eating or cooking, at the very least, eat those foods that provide you with a nutritiously balanced diet.

EASILY FATIGUED

- You may feel as if your body weighs much more than it used to. You drag yourself around from place to place.

- Problems in sleeping may occur which can cause even greater feelings of energy loss.

- You may find it an effort to perform daily activities.

- Which statements illustrate how you feel?

    "I feel like I'm old."

    "I have no motivation."

    "I can't last as long as I used to."

    "It is an effort to do the things I enjoy."

    "I have a hard time getting to sleep."

    "I awake in the middle of the night and can't get back to sleep."

    "I awake in the morning tired."

    "I can't get interested in anything."

    "I stay in bed for long periods of time to try and escape the pain."

Suggestions

One way to help with fatigue is to ask for help since many people would gladly assist if they knew what to do. Don't fall into the trap believing that "The best way to get something done is to do it myself." Permit yourself to let go of this belief and to delegate authority. Ask yourself questions such as:

"Does this task really need to be done?"
"Can I perform this task without doing it 'perfectly'?"
"Can I have someone else do this task?"

Try to engage in at least 25 minutes of exercise at least every other day, e.g., walking, jogging, biking, swimming, or any other aerobic activity. Consult with your physician. It may seem odd that an exercise program could help with fatigue. In fact people who engage in these activities three times a week for at least 25 minutes each time report significantly **more** energy and some degree of mood elevation after the fourth week into their program.

If you are not ready for an aerobic routine, then a lighter schedule could include: keeping track of your distance travelled each day using a pedometer, gardening, golf, yoga, walking the dog, or any other routine that gets you moving.

Sleep disruption is a common problem. Try these suggestions [11]:

As difficult as it might be, try to go to bed and rise at the same time each day.
Avoid caffeine after 5pm (this includes chocolate).
Try not to obsess about your lack of sleep—for most people it eventually improves. It takes a well-rested person 15-20 minutes to fall asleep.
Experts on sleep suggest that your bedroom should be cool, dark as possible and should be dimmed for several minutes prior to going to bed. This means turning off your computer screen, television, and overhead light.
Read something that will make you drowsy.
If you awaken during the night, do not turn on a light—it signals to your brain that it's time to wake up. A nightlight is fine but not an overhead light or a lamp.
Avoid oversleeping. Research has shown that sleeping more than 9 hours may be associated with as many health problems as short sleep.
Try taking a nap. Sleep research suggests that naps should either be 15-20 minutes or 90 minutes, not shorter or longer.
It is okay at times to use your bed as an escape. But, as time goes on, try to follow some of the other suggestions.

PHYSICAL PROBLEMS

- As a result of the death you may experience one or more of the following:

  Changes in sleeping patterns

  Tightness in chest

  Heart flutters

  Chills

  Constipation

  Diarrhea

  Headache

  Hot flashes

  Chills

  Increased blood pressure

  Knots in stomach

  Loss of sexual interest or heightened sexual feelings

  Lowered resistance to disease

  Nausea

  Nervousness

  Panic attacks

  Muscle Tension

- During the first year or two of the bereavement process, some people have more colds, flu, and other diseases than at other times in their life.

Suggestions

The grief-related physical reactions are not permanent and will decrease over time as your grief subsides.

If you haven't done so already, inform your doctor of your loss, and schedule a physical examination. Taking care of yourself is important. Keep in regular touch with your doctor to monitor your physical condition.

Even though the physical reactions are common symptoms of grief, it is critical to keep in mind that you do not "**deserve**" to suffer. Find acceptable methods to manage your physical ailments. While you may not be able to control the emotional reactions to loss, you can do something about many of the physical reactions.

A simple method of reducing tightness is to focus on the affected area, consciously tighten the muscles surrounding it, and release. Repeat this a few times until you can feel the decreased tension. Physical exercise can also help.

Learning relaxation techniques can help. You can purchase a relaxation CD. In addition, you can use the following relaxation technique:

> Close your eyes. Tighten and relax your forehead. Continue down your body as you tighten and relax each part from your head to your toes while saying "relax."

> Breathe—sit for a couple minutes, close your eyes and visualize your breath gently moving in and out of your of your nostrils.

If you obtain no relief from these methods, call your doctor.

SEX

- We humans are sexual beings. Sex is pleasurable.

- Because sex is, for many people, a moral issue, the decisions bereaved
  people make can be complicated with feelings of:
    embarrassment, guilt, inadequacy, fear, awkwardness, anxiety, confusion,
    emptiness, loneliness, shame, frustration, ambivalence, and regret.

- Grief can present a challenge to one's sexual feelings. Here are some examples:
    The death of a parent or sibling can affect a person's feelings about sex.
    A death can lead to a temporary suppression of sexual feelings and a
       lowered desire for physical affection.
    Alternatively, a death can be a factor in an increased desire for physical
       affection and sexual behavior.

- The death of a spouse or partner can be a challenge to one's sexuality.
    Death of a spouse, by definition, results in the loss of a sexual partner.
    It can bring up questions of dating that can produce feelings of guilt such
       as, "I'm cheating on him" as well as fear of sexually transmitted infections.
    Engaging in sexual relations after the death of a spouse or partner can
       result in feelings ranging from emptiness to euphoria.

- Grief may bring about mixed feelings about masturbation.

- The death of a child can complicate intimacy between a couple.
    Bereaved mothers have made statements such as:
    "Because this child came out of me, I just don't feel right having sex."
    "I am too lost and depressed to have any interest in physical intimacy."
    Some fathers have stated, "After the death of my child, my sex drive
       seemed to disappear for a time."
    Bereaved parents may feel guilty for wanting to engage in a
       pleasurable act at a time when one or both felt so low.
    Other parents felt that the continuation of their sexual intimacy helped
       nurture the closeness that they especially needed at the time.

Suggestions

Many younger people assume that, when a person reaches a "certain" age (pick one), sexual desire becomes nonexistent. The fact is, sexual feelings can be part of a person's life well into their elder years.

If you have a sexual partner, find a time to talk about sex. It is true that many people find that having sex is much easier than talking about it. Decide on a good time. Practice ahead of time on formulating a sentence to get things started, such as, "I want to talk for a few minutes about our lovemaking." Or "Can we talk for a little bit about sex?" In the discussion make sure each of you listens to one another's sexual concerns and needs.

If you are without a sexual partner, you have three options. Let's look at each.

1. *No Sex*. For some people, whether it is a decision to abstain or an accepted decline in one's sex drive, the death of one's partner could mean the end of their sexual life. For some people sexual intercourse is a sacred act. If this is your situation, and it feels right for you, then go with this feeling.

2. *Find Another Sexual Partner*. At some point after the death some people seek a person with whom to have a relationship—and the relationship ends up including sexual relations. Other people are not "looking" for a relationship, but it seems to find them. They may begin to notice that others are picking up on their status as a single person. For people who haven't dated in years, the decision to go out with someone can be a strange, awkward experience. For example, you might ask, "What is a date?" "Does it have to end with a sexual encounter?" "What about contraception?" "What about sexually transmitted diseases?" (There are more than 50, some of which—HIV, Herpes, Human Papilloma Virus—are incurable.)

It is *critical to have a plan* in order to later be clear about your physical and sexual boundaries. It could literally save your life. Therefore, prior to going out on a date, it is essential that you talk with a friend about *all* possible "what-ifs." Another way to think about this is to ask yourself, "If I do that, then what?" and "Then what?"....

3. *Masturbation*. This form of self-stimulation is another option. For some people this is foreign territory and for some it is a moral decision. For others it is a behavior they are comfortable with having done it in the past. However, if you are new to this, there are books on it and information on the Internet.

Understanding the Reaction of Others

CENTER-STAGE

- Since the death occurred, you may have the feeling that everyone is looking at you and that you are in the spotlight.

- People may be curious about the circumstances surrounding the death. Some may ask questions, while others may be reluctant to say anything they think may upset you — so they say nothing about the death, thinking that this is the best way to treat you.

- For a time after the death you may be given special status as a bereaved person and therefore excused from duties, forgiven for mistakes, and given a great deal of space. Many bereaved people report that this permission to be "weak" felt good. Others disliked the attention and felt "babied."

- Have the people around you implied that the time period allowed for this special status has expired? Do you now feel that you are (unfairly) expected to carry on your life much as you did prior to the death?

- Some bereaved people feel that the death, especially if it was a tragic one, is a reflection upon them as a person. For example, if the death was from AIDS or alcohol or drug problems, you may feel reluctant to share this with other people. If the death were a homicide or suicide, you or others may believe that this reflects poorly on you.

- Similarly, individuals who have lost children or grandchildren, people who lost a spouse, and siblings who lost a brother or sister are often avoided because others don't know what to say and don't know what to do and, as stated earlier, may somehow believe that death is contagious.

Suggestions

Realize that although a few people are curious for their own satisfaction about the events surrounding the death, it is likely that the majority of people who ask about details of the incident do so because they care about you and the person who died. It is a fact that whenever tragedies occur, our brain is programmed to ask, "Why?"

After you have told the story of the death a number of times, you may not feel like telling the next person who asks. However, it is true that having to tell the story numerous times will help move you through the denial process.

It is, however, your prerogative to say to the next person who enquires about the details of the death, "I don't feel like talking about it now (or at all)." In doing this, you might be careful not to push this person away by adding something like, "But I would like to go out to coffee with you."

Some people have chosen to put the death information on an Internet website as a way to inform others about the life of the person, manner of death, and needs of the family.

If the death was an accident, suicide, homicide, or drug-related, reporters may contact you for an interview. Beware: information you provide may not match the story published. You may want to consider refusing an interview at this time or appointing one family spokesperson to handle the media.

To those individuals who say nothing about the death you may want to say, "I want to say something: It is okay to talk about the death and about my loved one. It may be painful, but not talking about this is worse for me."

In dealing with the discrimination toward you stemming from the manner of death, you need to remember that you are a human being who has lost someone precious and those individuals who judge you based on the type of death are wrong. What is most important is that you do not direct any of these discriminatory behaviors to yourself and that you surround yourself with people who honor your right to grieve.

FEELINGS OF INTIMIDATION

- To feel intimidated is to feel pressured, bullied, coerced, or threatened.

- To experience grief from a death is hard enough. Some of the people you will have to deal with after the death may add to these grief reactions. Have you felt intimidated by any of the following people?

  Hospital Staff

  Medical examiner or coroner

  Funeral director

  Police

  Reporters

  The person or persons responsible for the death

  Friends and relatives of the person(s) responsible for the death

  People associated with the legal system

  Curious onlookers

  People who try to tell you what to do or how to feel

- You may feel unsettled at the method of questioning used to obtain information about events surrounding the death.

- You may feel intimidated by others in your search to obtain more information regarding the death.

Suggestions

The individuals involved with the death are trying to fulfill their roles. Your cooperation is what would help most. If they do not seem to recognize your feelings, tactfully let them know how you feel.

When in doubt as to your "right to know about information surrounding the death," ask. Keep asking until you are satisfied.

However, keep in mind that, if you are dealing with law enforcement agencies, they are not obligated to disclose any investigative records to the public or family of the deceased. Thus, material may be gathered as evidence and held until the investigation is concluded--which could take years.

At some point you may decide that you do not want any further information about the death. This is your choice.

Conversely, you may wish to know every last detail.

Finding the one helpful person in the office from the agency you are dealing with can make all the difference. Do not give up in finding this person.

It is totally acceptable to say, "no" to onlookers and reporters.

It is recommended that someone be with you as you deal with any of these agencies.

Find someone who can help you process and interpret information that is difficult to read and understand.

DEALING WITH LAW ENFORCEMENT

(In the case of a sudden death)

- After learning of the death, you may feel at times that the police are indifferent to your questions and concerns.

- You may feel upset at how unemotional they seem to be.

- You may provide them with what appears to you to be helpful information; and they may not act upon it for reasons that are unclear to you.

- You may feel frustrated at the pace that the information surrounding the investigation is sorted and acted upon.

Suggestions

There is no easy way to carry out the functions of investigating a sudden death, especially if it appears to be a homicide. A major problem is that the police have a limited amount of time they can spend on one case.

To help with this you may want to make a detailed record of events before and after the death. Include dates, locations, people, and events. Do not omit any details since they may later prove valuable.

Ask neighbors, friends, and family about anything they know or might have noticed concerning events surrounding the death. Small events can sometimes turn out to be significant.

In the case of an undetermined cause of death or an unsolved murder, the grief process may be especially nightmarish.

If there are times when the police seem uncooperative, it may help you to review the reactions and suggestions on Anger and on Feelings of Intimidation on pages 18 and 36.

Find a support group who understands what you are experiencing. Many communities offer a Victim Assistance program.

In the case of homicide, if the assailant is caught, and if there is to be a trial, be ready for a long, slow process that could take years.

If the death is reported in the media and you are overwhelmed with all the attention, give yourself permission to turn off the news.

If language or cultural barriers have made it difficult to interact with the authorities, find a trusted advocate who can bridge the barriers.

A FEELING THAT EVERYONE ELSE IS
CARRYING ON WITH "LIFE AS USUAL"

- At this time in your life the world may look different:

Artificial	Frightening
Indifferent	Callous
Insensitive	Cold
Uncaring	Dreary
Dull	Lonely

- You may find yourself angry, hurt, and astonished that, despite the fact that your life has totally changed, the rest of the world appears to operate just as it always has. Every day you see people going about their business as if nothing has changed.

- A common, but unexpressed feeling among bereaved people is their wish to say to the world, "Hey everybody, don't you understand that my life has been turned upside down and that everything is different?"

- You may have feelings of self-pity as you look at your life and feel sorry for what has happened to you. This is understandable.

- You will find yourself trying to put up with people who gush over their children, their grandchildren, their spouse, or other loved ones while you are coping with the death of yours.

- Even those people who know you well will not understand some of your grief reactions.

- You may find that you will receive support from some of the people around you during the first few months after the death. But, after a while some of your friends and family members may expect you to be "over" your loss. It is a common reaction by people in our society partly because they are concerned that you might "hang onto your grief too long." Because of their own discomfort watching your reactions to the death, they may want you to "get better."

- Another reason some people in your life don't want to be around you is because they do not want to deal with your pain or somehow think that it is *catching*.

Suggestions

Ask people to tell you stories of your loved one. You can write, audio or video them. A way to stimulate their memories is by asking them to remember:

> Embarrassing and funny moments
> Restaurants, meals, foods, smells
> Vacations, holidays, shopping, school
> Favorite songs, instruments
> Organizations, groups, clubs, scouts, sports, hobbies
> Outings, parties, picnics, concerts
> Favorite pets, toys, clothing, games, car
> Relationships with parents, siblings, friends
> Spiritual beliefs, church experiences, readings, prayers
> Support given to or received from your loved one
> Talents, idiosyncrasies, important values

Here is one way to get people to respond to your request for memories and stories:
> On the next holiday ask for written memories of your loved one when you send out cards or emails. You can use the list above.

On the other hand, be ready for some of the awkward things that well-meaning people say because they may not know what to say:

> *You'll get over it.*   *It was God's will.*   *He lived a long life.*
> *I know how you feel.*   *Don't worry.*   *It's for the best.*
> *At least ___ didn't suffer.* *Life goes on.*   *Things happen for a reason.*
> *Count your blessings.*   *You must accept it.* *It's time to move on.*
> *You can always remarry.*   *You are so strong.*   *You can have more children.*
> *If you **really** had faith in your religion (or God), you wouldn't feel this way.*

Remember, they are looking for words that they hope might ease your pain and they are not sure what else to say. Try to bear with them. For the special people who have helped you in your time of need consider writing a thank you note.

Here are examples of things you might say to those around you to garner support:
When you visit the gravesite, leave a note or some indication to say, "I was here."
Keep a picture of my loved one in your home.
Please remember the birthday.
Call me. Call me. Call me.

Continue to look for ways to get the kind of support you need.

SOCIETY'S REACTIONS

- While you are coping with the changes in your world, most of the rest of the world hardly notices.

- Research on how the media treat dying, death, and grief has revealed a "are-you-over-it" attitude [12]. In other words the message suggests that we need to move on, put the loss behind us, and heal.

- Examples of this are shown by the acronym CHARGE in which each letter represents a word often used by the media in response to grief, but seldom used by people in grief themselves. See if any of these terms sound familiar:

  Closure—as in: *Now that the body has been recovered the family can find closure.*

  Healed—as in: *Now that the funeral is over, the healing can begin*

  Acceptance—as in: *He can now accept the death of his son.*

  Recovered— as in: *Now that the couple has another child they can recover.*

  Get over it—as in: *In his volunteer work in helping others, he has found a way to get over his loss.*

  End it—as in: *With the trial over and the culprit behind bars, she can finally see an end to her grief.*

- While some religions have rituals that acknowledge the continuing struggle with the death of a loved one, society at large seems to have little tolerance for what it perceives as "prolonged grief." In a feeble attempt to somehow minimize the pain, clichés are offered.

- A common experience among bereaved people is the reaction by friends and strangers alike who express surprise that the person is *still* grieving, hasn't *moved on* with life, and even years later *continues* to have difficult days.

- Sometimes the only people who seem to tolerate this perceived "failure to *resolve* grief" are those who have had a shared experience. This appears to account for the success of grief support groups comprised of people who have had similar losses.

Suggestions

While it is easy to say, "Ignore society, forget the media, disregard what others say about your grief," it is clear that you, and others like you, are a minority.

You have accomplished an important step by reading this book. You understand that, while others may appear sure of their clichés, they don't get it—and probably won't get it unless they read about it or, unfortunately, experience it. A married woman once said to her newly widowed sister, "You had a good, long marriage. It's time to move on with your life." At the time the woman absolutely believed it was sound advice—until, that is, it happened to her a year later. Then she realized how empty her words sounded.

On the other hand, there will be people who will do things for you that will be so caring, so thoughtful that it may move you to tears. As you read this, think back on the kind, considerate, loving things that people have done for you since the death. As noted earlier, you might consider finding a small way to say "thank you" to these people.

Attending a support group with others who've experienced a similar loss can help in combating the tired expressions of an unaware populace. Online communities are also useful.

A common discussion in support groups involves the question, "How do you respond when a well-meaning person says something that takes you by surprise?" Here are some examples:

> When a bereaved father meets a stranger who asks, "So, do you have any children?" how should he respond?
> When a bereaved sibling meets an old friend who asks, "How's that brother of yours doing?" should he give the short version or long version of the tragic story?
> When a widow at two years is told by her very recently widowed friend, "I've begun dating and have met the nicest man." how can she react at the very moment her breath has been taken away?

There are no easy answers to these difficult questions. The most common answer is, "My response largely depends on how I feel at the moment."

How have bereaved people coped with society's lack of grief savvy? Here are some examples:

Educating oneself by reading articles and books on the bereavement process.
Attending support group meetings.
Taking a class.
Finding a friend who is a good listener.
Locating a counselor who knows about grief.
Exploring reliable sites on the Internet that include chat rooms, eBooks, and short articles.

A NEED TO TALK IT OUT

- At times do you feel no one understands?

- Because it is difficult for some people to watch your grief in all its intensity and duration, you may experience the departure of people who were once close to you.

- For a period of time after the death some people will be there to help you; but, as time goes on, you will likely find that fewer people will be as available to you.

- Do you find that you want to talk about your loved one more than people are willing to listen?

- Do people show their discomfort with your grief reactions?

- As time goes by you will see that more people will refrain from bringing up the death or the name of your loved one. It may seem as if they have either "forgotten" or don't wish to discuss it. Some may even believe that it would be "too upsetting" to talk about this person. They let their own discomfort get in the way and remain silent, or worse, they leave you alone in your grief.

- If you answered "Yes" to some of the questions on this page, ask yourself, "What can I do about this?" Suggestions are on the next page.

Suggestions

Be honest with others, yet be aware that some people will respond negatively to your frankness. Let them. As time goes on, support people will mistakenly believe that you need less help rather than more because most people do not understand grief reactions. Loan them this book.

As best you can, tell people exactly how you feel. Even though many may not be supportive, you may be pleasantly surprised at the response. Try this with more than one person. Say to a friend, "Do you have time for me now, or in the next few days when we can talk for awhile about the death? I need someone to just listen to me for a while. You don't have to say much or try to fix it. There's nothing to solve. I just need an ear."

A list of suggestions for being a good listener*
(Share this list with your friends.)

When listening to a friend in grief, a good listener:
1. Lets the person do most of the talking
2. Tries to refrain from:
   Analyzing   Interrupting
   Judging   Minimizing feelings
   Telling the person what to do and how to feel
3. Permits awkward silence
4. Asks, "What kind of thoughts have you been having?"
5. Paraphrases – that is, after listening intently for a time, summarizes what the person has just said; and does this only once or twice during the session.
6. Is encouraging by helping to explore alternatives by asking, "What else can you do?" and assists in compiling a list of possible courses of action.
7. Mentions the deceased person frequently, says the name, and brings up stories.
8. Calls on the bereaved person *more frequently* over the months and years.
9. Remembers that grief cannot be "fixed."
10. Shows caring in a variety of ways.

In summary, a good listener permits the sharing of grief without interrupting, judgment, or trying to fix it.

*For a more complete list of listening suggestions, find on the Internet: How to be a good listener to a friend, "Bob Baugher YouTube."

BEING ALONE VS. BEING INVOLVED

- At times you may have a desire to limit your interactions with others. People in your life may misinterpret your temporary desire to be alone as a rejection.

- Yet, at other times you may feel a desperate need to be with others. Your loneliness becomes unbearable. The daily absence of your precious loved one seems more than you can endure. You wonder how you can go on like this.

- For a time after the death you may want to talk about your grief only with people who have had an identical loss. For example, one woman wanted at first to talk only to bereaved people who, like herself, lost a 20 year-old son. Later she extended herself to bereaved parents who lost children of other ages.

- As time passes the realization hits you again and again (and again) that you no longer have what others have or you don't belong anymore to the groups of people with whom you once had commonalities. This may be especially painful when you are around others who have what you don't. For example, widowed people may feel like a "fifth wheel" around their married friends. Grandparents may find it hard to hear friends' stories of grandchildren when one of theirs is no longer alive.

- Bereaved people sometimes look with envy at people who enjoy interactions with their own loved ones. As one woman whose brother died put it, "I watch my friends chatting and laughing with their brothers and it hurts me. They don't really understand how lucky they are to have their brother." A man whose mother died admitted, "When I see someone my age with an older person, I want to go up to them and say, 'Oh, is this your mother (or father)? Parents are precious. You're lucky to have yours.'"

- The loss may leave you feeling more lonely than you ever have in your life.

Suggestions

If you experience a desire to be alone, tell people (especially children) that you need space. Go somewhere by yourself and, if you feel the need, have a good, long cry. Do this as often as you wish. Whether it be physical space or emotional space, solitude is sometimes necessary.

Don't keep your grief to yourself just because you don't want to "trouble" anyone. When you want to be touched, held, or hugged, tell people. If your friends were in your predicament, you would want to help them, wouldn't you? They probably feel the same way. Admitting that you are lonely may be embarrassing; and taking the risk of being rejected by another person is difficult, especially if you have been rejected recently. The alternative is to be left alone with your grief. Reach out, despite your setbacks. You deserve to be helped at a time like this. Someday you may be able to return the favor.

Make a list of possible support people. Some people can help by just "being there" to give you emotional support — such as being a good listener. Other people can better help you by doing things for you, such as repairs, errands, and favors, while others can be supportive by sending you helpful information.

As you are well aware, you cannot stop the behaviors of people around you who still have a partner, sibling, parent, friend, or child. It is difficult to observe others living a life you do not have. Your feelings are normal. Talk with others who've experienced a similar loss to gain insight into how they have coped.

Bereavement support groups can be very helpful. Some people have reported that they would not be alive today were it not for their support group. Other people feel that they would do better to work on their grief without group involvement. Answering "yes" to the following questions indicates that you might benefit from a support group:

Do I want to find out more about grief from other people?

Am I ready to get out of the house and attend a meeting?

Do I have a desire to listen to the grief experiences and coping strategies of other people?

Am I ready to tell my story?

Is there a support group in my community?

Would an online support group better suit me?

ESCAPE

- How well are you managing your grief?

- Drinking alcohol or using other drugs may seem like an easy way to forget and a way to escape.

- When the effects wear off, the memory and feelings will return waiting to be worked **on**.

- Other problems with coping that may temporarily feel like an escape are shown by:

  Overeating

  Overspending

  Sleeping the day away

  Pushing people away

  Moving to another location to avoid facing the reality

  Entering too quickly into a new love relationship

  Overworking (workaholism) at the job to avoid facing the reality

  Excessive exercising

  Over-traveling (constant avoidance of home)

  Risk-taking

  Gambling

Suggestions

Watch your impulses and as much as possible try to imagine the outcome of your actions before you jump into anything. An impulsive behavior may feel good temporarily, but ask yourself, "If I do this now, what will happen next? And then what? And then what?" Then take this "*then what*" thinking to its logical conclusion.

Do not stop yourself from thinking about the death, the loss, the pain, and the person. However, continuing to dwell on the death so much that you cannot perform your daily duties is not healthy. Again, find a balance.

Sometimes bereaved people cope with their unbearable pain by imagining that the person is not dead but instead away on a trip. For example, widowed people report that they sometimes imagine their spouse is at work, on a business trip, or visiting a friend; and bereaved parents sometimes imagine that their child is staying with relatives, at the mall, or away at school. At the same time they are doing this, the bereaved person also knows deep down that their loved one is dead. It is simply a common, temporary escape from the horrible reality that this person will *never* return.

Although escaping and avoiding all the reminders of the death of your loved one is not healthy, there are other things that you can try to do—even for a few minutes—so as not to have to constantly face the harsh reality of the death. As you well know, distractions such as the following can help, but they only help temporarily:

> Keeping busy around the house
> Helping someone in need
> Working on a hobby or something creative
> Watching television or a movie or surfing the Internet
> Reading (However, most people find it hard to concentrate.)
> Socializing and going on outings
> Recreational activities

Try to avoid changing your residence during the first year after the death. Most experts agree that it is not wise to move during this time even though well-meaning friends and relatives encourage you to do so. Wait. You can always move later.

If possible, wait at least a year on making major decisions in your life, whether it is a major purchase, dating, having another child, or getting remarried. As incredibly difficult as it might be right now, try to resist doing these things even though it may seem like the best thing to do at the moment. Wait. You can always decide later.

Thought-Related Reactions

QUESTIONING YOURSELF AND OTHERS

• Common questions include:

Why did this happen?

Why did this happen to me?

How could this have happened?

Who is responsible?

Why did God let this happen?

How can I continue to live like this?

What is wrong with me?

What good is living?

Why didn't I die instead?

How can I live with this unbearable pain?

Why don't people understand me?

Why do I get to go on living?

Where is my loved one now?

What is life all about?

When will I get better?

What is going to happen to me?

Suggestions

It is highly frustrating to realize that some of these questions have no clear answers.

Questions of suicide, homicide, and unknown causes of death can be especially difficult because no one can ever truly understand what went on in a person's mind prior to the event.

Most bereaved people come to realize that "Sometimes, there is no justice in the world." They arrive at the hard truth that all types of people die before their time, including the good, the young, and the innocent. This realization can alter a person's world-view.

Some bereaved people engage in what has been called "magical thinking" in which they come up with their own scenario in an attempt to answer one or more of the questions on the previous page. For example, the death of a child may lead a parent to answer the question, "Why did this happen?" by deciding that this was punishment from God for a past sin. Similarly, a child may come to believe that her father died because she had said, "I hate you" months before the death. If you find yourself engaging in such thinking, it is important to take three steps:

1. Share your thoughts with someone who can be a good listener.
2. Ask, "Would the person who died want me to think this way?"
3. Ask, "What would I say to a friend who may have similar thoughts?"

If you are unclear about the actual cause of death or any events surrounding the death, contact the hospital or Medical Examiner's Office (coroner). As noted earlier, you may want to make a personal appointment and come with a list of questions. You have a right to ask.

Many people turn to their belief in God to help them cope with the overwhelming pain. Their belief provides them with a sense of comfort in the midst of pain and confusion. Other people feel an increased distance from their previous spiritual beliefs. Questions of one's spirituality or religion can be discussed with a member of the clergy or other people who are willing to listen.

You may get answers to some of your questions someday.

Another possibility is that the answers are A+B+C...+M. The M is for mystery. That is, you may find partial answers, but it may happen that there remains an "M" for answers that will frustratingly never come.

WORRY

You certainly have a right to worry because a terrible thing happened in your life.

In addition to the death, you may have also experienced financial loss. You worry about your economic future.

When people say to you, "Don't worry about that." does it stop you from worrying? Of course not. Because of this death, your brain has a need to think about things over and over and over. And worry is part of the process. However, worry has limits.

Worry is our *self-talk about the future*. Worry can be a catalyst or a catastrophe.

How is worry different from anxiety?Anxiety = worry + emotionality (physical arousal)

One cause of worry is the inability to tolerate uncertainty. Worry is an attempt to decrease our discomfort or our inability to control a situation. When a person is prevented or discouraged from worrying there is often an emotional rebound in which the person feels *worse*.

Worrying can be productive. It can help us plan for the future by anticipating possible outcomes and taking preventive steps.

Worrying becomes a problem when it moves to a level of catastrophizing and it interferes with our activities of daily living; and all we're doing is ruminating— thinking about something over and over and over.

Reasons why we worry:
1. **Punishment Cause**: We didn't worry about something and—bam—it happened. In this case we got punished (blindsided) for not worrying. Then we say, "I should've anticipated this happening. Then it wouldn't have been this bad. In the future I won't be blindsided again."
2. **Generalized Learning**: A single event occurred and we then generalize it to other potential events. "My mother died suddenly. Now I'm worried that everyone else I care for can suddenly die too."
3. **Reinforced Worrying**: We worry about many things; and 99% never happen. Then, when the one event out of 100 happens we say, "See, it was good that I worried. I somewhat prepared myself for it." Or to put it another way: Many people are less anxious when they worry as if they are somehow preparing for some terrible event.
4. **Social Worrying**: Other people around us are worrying, so we join in.
5. **Proxy Worrying:** Sometimes we worry because others around us aren't.

Suggestions

Four Critical Suggestions from worry experts:

1. *Write down your worries*. You must get them on paper where you can see them.
2. *Find a good time to worry*. Prior to going to sleep is not the time. If you start to worry in bed, say to yourself, "I can worry about this tomorrow."
3. *Find a specific place in which to worry*. Let it be your exclusive worry place. Make it a place where you typically don't spend much time e.g. your porch, in one corner of your bedroom, in the backseat of your car, in your closet.
4. *Find a good listener* who can work with you on this.

Do you catastrophize? Catastrophizing occurs when our imagination runs away from us and we absolutely believe the *worst* could happen. Because we've had catastrophes in our life such as this one, we may believe they could happen again. Mere possibilities of tragic events now seem more likely.

As a result of this thinking you may have become overprotective and your caring may be smothering other people in your life.

Don't believe everything you think is a motto to live by.

For the worries you can do something about, break them down into Action Steps such as:

1. What do I need to do about this worry?
2. Who do I need to contact about this worry?
3. What are the things I need to say to the person who is the center of this worry?
4. What is stopping me from taking care of this worry and what can I do about it?

For worries over which you have no control, here are three suggestions in addition to the first three listed above:

1. Imagine the worst possible outcomes of a particular worry. Go ahead and consider every conceivable negative result. As practice, take one of your highest worries and answer the question: *What are all the terrible things that would happen if this worry were to come true?*
2. Then, ask "What is my estimate of *how likely* that each of these events will happen?"
3. The last step is to say to yourself: *If any of these events do happen, I will deal with it in ways such as talking it out with a good listener, prayer, exercise, counseling, meditation, journaling.*

DIFFICULTY WITH CONCENTRATION

- When a crisis comes in the door, concentration often goes out the window.

- Problems in memory and difficulty in reading, listening, and paying attention to detail are common. One major reason is due to lack of sleep. A brain that lacks sleep will compensate for it during the day by blanking out for a few seconds at a time, perhaps hundreds of times a day, sometimes without the person's awareness.

- Another reason for concentration problems stems from uncontrolled flooding of visual images in the mind:
  The face or full body of the person who died
  The dying process
  The death
  The funeral, casket, flowers, cremation
  Flashes of moments with your loved one

- Other problems in concentration are due to the heightened stress and emotional reactions in your life stemming from all of the overwhelming problems the death has brought.

- You may find that things distract you more easily than before.

- You may not feel like going to work, school, and meetings.

- You may find yourself forgetting:
  Appointments
  People's names
  What you want while it is in front of you. For example, staring at an item on the shelf in the grocery store and not remembering why you wanted it in the first place.
  How to perform activities
  What you were saying in conversation
  Where you put things (Some bereaved people call this the "here- after" problem. That is, they set out to find something and when they get there, their mind goes blank and they ask themselves, "What am I *here* after?")

Suggestions

Most bereaved people report that, after several months (for some people, after a year or more), their ability to concentrate begins to improve, if only a little.

If you can, find ways to compensate for your difficulty with concentration. For example, you can inform the people around you to regularly double check your daily tasks that require detailed attention.

Do not rely on your memory. Presume you are going to forget things. Write notes to yourself for appointments and post them in places where you cannot miss them, such as the refrigerator, front door, on (not in) your purse or wallet, on your car steering column, or on your computer or phone.

Ask friends to help you with some of your tasks. Remember, asking for help does not make you a weak person. Instead it indicates that you know how to take care of yourself as you go through a highly difficult time in your life.

Many people have chosen to continue their work schedule because it helped keep them occupied during their grief period. Other people choose to take a leave of absence in order to deal with their problems without the added stress of employment duties.

Because of your distractibility, you may be more prone toward accidents. It may be helpful to engage in some self-talk while driving, to keep you more alert. For example, say to yourself as you start your car on a rainy day, "It's slick out today. Keep it under 35."

Find ways to organize your priorities:

> Make a list of *Things to Do*.

> Rewrite the list in priority order.

> Keep a calendar of appointments.

Keep a diary or journal. As noted earlier, it may be difficult at a time like this, but it can later provide a therapeutic perspective as you move through this process.

Doing the things suggested here will not "weaken" your brain's concentration ability. While at times it may feel embarrassing to forget things and to have to post notes to yourself, do whatever you can to maintain a bit of order in this crazy time of your life. You are coping with grief. Be patient with yourself.

DREAMS AND FEELINGS OF PRESENCE

- Experts on dreams tell us that the average person:
    Has an average of 3-6 dreams per night
    Does not remember most dreams
    Has dreams that consist of random combinations of experienced events,
        imagined memories, or anticipated future events
    Has dreams that are not clearly interpretable

- Some common themes of death-related dreams are:
    The person is alive and you are not surprised by this
    The person is alive, you are surprised, and:
        The person helps you make sense of the situation or
        You are confused in the dream at their state of living.
    The person is present, but somehow dead in the dream.
    The person appears younger or older in the dream.

- Another common occurrence among bereaved persons is to feel that a form of
  "contact" had been made. Reports of these experiences can be put into four categories:

    Visual —   seeing the person standing in the kitchen or at the foot of the bed

    Auditory—hearing the voice of the person or hearing one's name called when
    no one else is around

    Tactile — feeling the person's bodily presence, such as in bed or feeling a hand
    on one's shoulder or feeling tapping on the arm

    Olfactory—smelling a scent associated with the person

- The fact that these type of reports by bereaved people are so common suggests
  that this experience can be considered normal. In addition, the reported experiences do not typically occur when the person has been asleep or is about to fall
  asleep. Both the dreams and reports of a "contact" occur on irregular bases.

  Some people believe that contact has been made through signs from their loved one:
    Lights flickering or other electrical occurrences
    The appearance of butterflies, birds, animals, flowers, rainbows or other objects
    Special songs
    Items moved

Suggestions

If you have not had a dream or other experience, this does not mean that you miss this person any less than people who have many of these experiences. You may feel left out and wonder why it has not happened to you. What follows are suggestions that may help.

Although most people remember few of their dreams, there is something you can do. Keep a paper and pen or recorder next to your bed and the moment you awaken during the night or the following morning ask yourself, "What did I dream?" Because dreams are not typically stored in our long-term memory, they fade fairly quickly upon awakening. Therefore, do not rely on your memory—write it down or talk it.

If you wish to increase the likelihood of having a dream of the person who died, do the following: try repeating as you are falling asleep, "I am going to have a pleasant dream about _____."

Sometimes writing or "talking out" a dream can help. At other times it does little good. If you have a negative dream concerning your loved one, do not assume there is some deep, hidden message at play. While dreams often have a story-content to them, most experts agree that dreams defy clear and unambiguous interpretation. Don't let someone else interpret your dream. Instead ask yourself the *one* important dream question, which is, "With this dream, what is my mind trying to tell me?" If no answer emerges, then there is no answer.

Have you had recurring nightmares? A suggested way of dealing with this is to follow these steps:

1. Write down the dream in detail
2. At the frightening part write a change to the story to make it become positive.
3. When your head hits the pillow, practice the revised dream in your mind.

There is no clear answer to the question of reported contacts between the bereaved and their deceased loved ones. One side of the argument states that people in grief are so desperate for comfort from the intense pain they are experiencing that their mind inadvertently creates conditions or notices events that are interpreted as "contact" with the person who died. The other side argues that, to the person having the experience, the contact feels very "real" and unlike any dream or waking experience.

BELIEFS AND RITUALS

- One of the most difficult questions surrounding a death is "Why did this happen?"

  Meaning-making following a death has been said to be an important, central process in grieving [13, 14, 15]. Below are some of the categories of reasons that people have used to help make meaning after a death:

  Destiny—It was fate. Nothing could have prevented it.

  Heredity—The person's genetic background contributed to the death. If true, this can be a source of worry for blood relatives who may have inherited the same tendencies.

  God—Spiritual or religious beliefs provide an answer.

  Payback—The death is some sort of punishment for negative behaviors performed by the person who died or by the survivor.

  Mental Disorder—The person had a psychiatric problem that somehow led to the death.

  Curse—Similar to Payback, but the survivor feels that the death was due to a supernatural power

  Life-style—Risky life-style decisions were to blame: drug or alcohol use, smoking, eating problems, risk-taking behaviors, or stress-related problems.

  Suicide—For reasons that survivors will never fully understand, the person carried out a life-ending plan.

  Unlucky—An unfortunate event led to the death.

  Negligence—The death occurred because of a mistake by the person, a third party, or worse, by the survivor.

  Senseless–Some deaths occur for reasons that make absolutely no sense.

- Do you engage in rituals, that is, faithfully followed patterns of behavior? Examples are:

  Visiting a certain place on a regular basis, such as the gravesite or bedroom

  Looking at, carrying, or touching an object such as a picture, article of clothing, jewelry, or memento

  Listening to a song repeatedly

  Working on a project in the name of the person who died

Suggestions

After answering the question, "Why did this happen?" answer these questions:

How did you arrive at your conclusion?

Would it help if you spoke to someone?

What would your loved one say about your answer?

What have you learned from this death?

As a result of the death, are you going to alter your own life-style in some way?

If you believe that the death occurred because of some "payback" for something you did, you might be susceptible to feelings of guilt. You may want to reread the section on Guilt, page 12.

The feeling of being cursed is common among people who experienced more than one death within a short time or for those whose loved one died in a tragic way. You may want to find other people who have had similar experiences. Listening to others can help you understand that tragedy can strike anyone and that it was not due to a "curse."

Rituals can produce positive results because they can provide you with a clear set of prescribed actions that can ease the grief.

However, rituals can also have negative effects if skipping them a time or two, either purposely or accidently, will lead to guilt, anxiety, and feeling that the memory of the deceased has been "betrayed." Ask yourself:

If I skip this ritual, will I feel as if I have done something "wrong?"

Is this ritual keeping me from doing the things in my life that I need to do?

If the person who died could say anything about the rituals, what would it be?

Should I talk to someone about this?

Is there anything else I should do to obtain similar results without having to rely strictly on this ritual?

Bereaved people report that, as time goes by, they do not feel as compelled to maintain the same rituals that they followed during the early part of their bereavement process.

SELF-IDENTITY—WHO AM I NOW?

- "Who am I now?" is a common question asked by millions of people whose lives have been forever changed by a death.

- When you think back on your life, perhaps you view it in terms of "before the death" and "after the death." Before the death you were one person. Now, you are a different person.

- **A Bereaved Spouse.** Whether the death was sudden or due to a chronic illness, people whose spouse or partner dies are suddenly thrust into widow(er)hood. If you are widowed, think back when you first filled out an application that read, *married* or *single*, did you hesitate? How could you be single? How could you live with someone for so many years and one day be alone? One woman put it this way, "When the death occurred, I went from one world into a totally different world just like that."

- **Bereaved Parents or Grandparents**. The death of a child or grandchild leaves family members forever changed. If this is you, you have seen other children grow and move on with their lives knowing that your family will never experience the celebrations that other families are fortunate enough to have. People you thought were friends began to fade from your life, some because they mistakenly believed that the death of a child is "catching;" others because they see how death has transformed you into a different person.

- **Bereaved Sibling.** If you have experienced the death of a brother or sister, you have seen life-altering changes in both you and your family. As you know, sibling relationships can be complex and can consist of various combinations of: love, rivalry, friendship, or alienation. With death may come issues of unfinished business, guilt, and anger. In addition, you may have been left to live in the shadow of your deceased brother or sister while also helplessly watching your family forever changed.

- **Bereaved Child.** Research on the death of a parent during childhood has documented innumerable effects on the developing child. The resiliency of children along with the support of caring adults can go a long way in buffering the effect of parental loss. The death of a parent in adult years is often minimized as the natural course of life events. Has this happened to you? Yet, for many adults the death of a parent is experienced as a significant loss. Whatever the age, the death of a father or mother can alter the answer to the identity question, "Who am I now?"

Suggestions

For many people the change in identity is one of the most difficult issues in grief. If you are having the common recurring thoughts listed below, let them come up again and again until they begin to subside. Despite the pain, allow yourself to feel the grief over these losses of identity. If you are like many people, these thoughts will take a long time before they aren't part of your daily mantra:

"I want her back." Or "I want him back."

"I want my old life back."

"I wish I could turn back the clock."

"I don't like my life."

The fact that you are a different person is a harsh reality. If you look at this from the perspective that everyone has hundreds of personality traits that comprise self-identity, it is clear that some of your personality traits have changed significantly while others may have changed a little and others have remained much the same.

Think for a minute, how *are* you the same? As an example, ask yourself, "Am I still the same as I was prior to the death in any of the following traits?"

Conscientiousness

Agreeableness

Extraversion

Trustworthiness

Openness to new experiences

Nervousness

Resilient to setbacks

Need for control

Rock of the family

Tendency to ask for help

Hopeful

Next, ask yourself, "How am I different in these areas?" The point is, parts of you have forever changed.

Finding people and information that can help you negotiate this new world is the best thing you can do for yourself right now.

WHAT AM I GOING TO DO NOW?

- Do you feel helpless? Uncertain about your future?

- Some days you will awaken in the morning and, for a second or two, you may forget that your loved one is gone forever. . . and then it hits you and again the harsh reality of the loss washes over you.

- One of the most difficult things for bereaved people to cope with are the daily reminders that tell them their lives have changed forever.

- The intense levels of pain feel like they will never stop. They will.

- You may not feel like selling or giving away your loved one's belongings.

- If the person who died is a spouse or partner, a major issue may be what to do with your wedding ring. Some people continue to wear it until they die, others later decide to:

    Put it on their other finger

    Wear it around their neck

    Put it away

    Go to a jeweler and have the two melted together

- You feel like you are moving on with life even though you don't want to. The weeks have turned into months, and you were afraid of the months turning into years. The day your loved one died is forever part of your life. Even though you may not have wanted to, the next day you got up. Then another day passed and then another. And, here you are today, reading this book, perhaps wondering where the time went. How could you still be living your life without your precious person in it?

Suggestions

Someone you love has died. To say that you must go on with your life may sound simplistic, perhaps cruel. Even though you may feel that life isn't worth living, it is important to continue to live even though your heart isn't in it.

A valuable piece of advice comes from bereaved people who know what it took to help with their grief. It is: **One day at a time**.

Don't forget this advice. Many people say that this was their motto that helped them survive. For some people, especially in the early months of grief, it was more like: One *moment* at a time.

Regarding visiting the gravesite or special place, some people choose not to at all, others visit once in a while, and yet others choose to visit often and continue to do so for years. It is okay to do this as long as you are not spending so much time there that you are neglecting the rest of your life.

As time goes by, despite your pain, begin to rebuild your life by taking risks to again involve yourself with the world. Enjoying your life doesn't mean that you are forgetting this precious person. You deserve happiness.

As noted earlier, It is okay to wait before you decide what to do with your loved one's belongings. You do not have to rush into this. Do not let well-meaning friends and relatives convince you to make decisions you are not ready to make. For example, many bereaved people keep clothing items because they can smell the scent of their loved on them; and some people even sleep with these items.

Some people wait for months — some for years. Others begin to sort out the belongings a few months after the death, keeping things, giving things away, selling some things, and putting the "undecided" items in boxes. They then make an agreement with all family members that the boxes will be reopened on the one-year anniversary, or they may decide to wait longer.

As stated in the Introduction, the variety of suggestions in this book reminds us that coping with grief involves many courses of action. Because the reactions listed on the previous pages do not appear all at once during the grieving process, you may find it helpful to refer to this book now and then, rereading different sections.

In the past few years some excellent material has been published concerning the grief process. Ask people who have experienced your type of loss to recommend helpful reading material.

GRIEF IN THE LONG-TERM

- Is thinking about the future confusing and frightening? One reason may be because the future is seen as a time when your loved one may not be as clearly remembered. Somehow it seems that the space of time will put a distance between you and the person you lost. Another reason is because you probably think that you cannot go on, and the future does not seem as clear and positive as it used to be.

- Bereaved people unanimously report that they do not gradually get better on a day-to-day basis. Instead the process of getting better has been compared to an involuntary ride on a runaway roller coaster:

  It is out of your control.

  It involves frequent difficult climbs and many sudden drops.

  What's around the next turn is unpredictable.

  Getting off is all you can think about.

- Holidays and birthdays are difficult because of the flood of memories surrounding such events. Reminders are everywhere. The first birthday and other special occasions can be especially painful. Does this sound familiar? This person should be here, just like last year, laughing and enjoying the day. The person's life feels frozen at the age of death. You continue to mourn "what could have been" had your precious loved one continued to live.

- Anniversary dates related to the death are difficult as well. (Many people are reluctant to even use the word "anniversary," since it commonly applies to something positive.) For many people the date of the death is initially noticed by the day of the week, later by date of the month, and finally by the year. For example, if a man's mother died on Friday the 24th, he will likely notice each Friday as it comes up and say, "It's been two weeks now . . . it's been six weeks" and so on. As the weeks turn into months, he begins to notice the Fridays less and each 24th of the month more.

- As the years go on you may continue to focus on dates and events that *would have been*. For example, a parent who cries on the day that would have been graduation day; or a woman who cries on her daughter's wedding day because her husband should be walking his daughter down the aisle.

Suggestions

Long-term bereaved people want you to know that you never *get over* the death, you *get different*. You will always be a different person for what you have gone through with this loss. Some people have eventually called their different life a "new normal." Others don't like the term.

Whenever you hear people say that they have experienced a similar loss, you will know much of what they are saying. However, as you well know, your grief experience and methods of coping are unique.

You might ask, "Is there a way to avoid the roller coaster ride altogether?" Some experts believe that avoiding the bereavement process leads to future emotional and physical problems. Other experts have found that there are some people who seem to do quite well without experiencing the intense emotions of grief. Whatever you do, be patient with yourself.

Some people try to keep holiday customs and traditions much the same as before the death. Other people alter some aspects of it, and still others totally change the holiday. Whatever you do is fine, as long as you have told your plans to other people. During the first years, many people report that having some type of birthday acknowledgment for their loved one was the right thing to do.

Have you found that the anticipation of the anniversary date is more stressful than the actual date? Consider the next important date and have a plan for what you will do that day. If you happen to miss one of the important dates, be careful not to assume that you are "forgetting" your loved one. Missing a date is not a measure of your love.

For most people, hitting the one-year point is a major milestone. It shows that they made it through the most difficult year of their life. Some people report that during the first year they believed that, by going through every important date once, their lives would somehow improve. However, as they moved into their second and third year and beyond, they put this belief into perspective. Grief work is slow. While the grieving continues and the yearning is present, things do get better.

Remember: One day—or one moment—at a time.

RELATING TO MY LOVED ONE

- For some people the death of their loved one involves:
  Saying "good-bye"
  Leaving the person behind
  Severing the relationship
  Feeling as if the person no longer exists

- For others the death leads them to become aware that they relate to this person in new ways. Here are examples.

  Some people:

      Speak to their loved one frequently throughout the day. Others do so, ranging from a couple times a day to once a week or month to once or twice a year.

      Some people speak aloud to this person. Others do so silently.

      Feel the presence of their loved one on a continuous basis

      Experience intermittent feelings of contact

      Encounter moments of connecting with this person a few times over the years

- People across many cultures have a practice whereby they consult with a deceased party in the context of making an important decision. If you have done this, you are in the company of many people.

- Let's review some of the ways that people feel or stay connected:
  Looking at pictures or videos
  Wearing clothing or jewelry
  Engaging in activities or behaviors related to their loved one
  Performing a ritual
  Going to meaningful places
  Praying
  Acknowledging important days in this person's life
  Keeping meaningful items linked to this person
  Working on a project in honor of their loved one
  Telling or listening to stories of the person's life

Unique Grief Reactions Brought on by Sudden Death

Death as a result of an accident, murder, suicide, or unknown cause can create complex grief reactions. Most causes of death involve a warning. A sudden death, however, tends to increase the complexity of the bereavement process. Many factors add to the burden of grief:

1. We have no time to prepare for the event. There is a longer period of shock and denial.

2. The person who died is referred to as a "victim."

3. When we think of our loved one, the injuries they received may hurt and sadden us. At the same time, however, we may feel a sense of relief that death freed the person from pain.

4. The fact that death is a matter of public record may detract from our wish for privacy in a time of grief.

5. An investigation by authorities who ask questions about events surrounding the death may bother us, but may also bring us closer to understanding the cause of it.

6. There may be directed anger and resentment toward those whom you feel are responsible for the death.

7. There may be difficulty in accepting the guilty party as human in cases where a willful act was committed that resulted in death. For many survivors this process is a difficult one that challenges their ability to forgive.

8. There may be mixed feelings toward an unknown, destructive force in the case where the real reason for the death is unclear.

9. Anyone who feels even remotely responsible for the death might experience feelings of guilt.

10. Helplessly watching your other loved ones mourn the death—or in some cases, appear to be relatively unaffected by the death—can add to your own feelings of grief.

AS YOU MOVE ON:
THREE TYPES OF CONSTRUCTIVE COPING [16]

Coping with death involves continuous, moment-to-moment responses to over-whelming thoughts and emotions and to the gradual realization that your life is forever changed. With this in mind, here are three positive ways that people tend to react to setbacks in their lives. These three types of constructive coping will provide a review of some of the reactions and suggestions discussed in this book.

Appraisal-Focused Constructive Coping

Problem-Focused Constructive Coping

Emotion-Focused Constructive Coping

I. Appraisal Focused Constructive Coping

The word "appraisal" refers to the methods we use to evaluate our present situation. See if any of these coping techniques applies to you.

Watch your negative self-talk

In coping with your grief, do you find yourself using words such as: *should, need to, must, always, never, everyone, no one*? Do you say to yourself, "I'm a failure." or "I must be perfect." or "I will feel this way forever"? Your job is to catch your-self when these words and phrases come up and replace it with less negative self talk such as, "Okay. I need to ease up a bit. My loved one would not want me to be so hard on myself."

Use humor

It may sound strange to consider humor when you are hurting so bad at this point in your life. Laughter is seen by some bereaved people as disparaging the memory of the person who died. However, despite your pain, isn't it true that your loved one would want you to find laughter in your life again?

Re-interpret the loss

The devastation you may be feeling is real. People might try to ease your grief with empty phrases. How death influences your life is your choice. You can let it destroy you. You can become a bitter person. You can give up on life or you can look back and be eternally grateful that this wonderful human being was in your life. Yes, you wanted more time; but now you can begin to appreciate how fortunate you were to be loved by this precious person.

If your relationship with this person had problems, you can still find ways to work on them and become whole again. One important way of re-interpreting a loss, is to ask yourself, "What did I learn from this death?" If the death has left you with painful, unfinished business, counseling can be very helpful.

When you are ready, ask yourself, "How am I going to live out my life in a way that I feel good about myself?" "What goals do I need to pursue?" "What places do I need to visit? "Who needs my help?"

II. Problem-Focused Constructive Coping

Make a list of troubles in your life

This is an important first step. Of course many cannot be resolved—but write them out, nonetheless. Many people in grief do not like this suggestion because their troubles feel so overwhelming. A common response is, "What's the use?" You may ask a friend to help you with the list. Once you see the list of your problems in writing, circle the ones over which you have some degree of control. Next, with your friend's help, generate as many alternative courses of action as you can. Then, decide on the action steps for each one.

Ask for help

Your next step is to put aside your pride and take the risk to ask people directly for help in carrying out your action list. Can you do this? A support person may simply be a cheer leader or someone who can help keep you on track.

III. Emotion-Focused Constructive Coping

Find a good listener

Finding that one caring person who can be a good listener is a critical step. For good listening suggestions refer back to page 45.

Keep a journal.

As noted earlier, putting your feelings down in writing, on a computer, or on a voice recorder is a powerful way to cope with grief. It not only gets out the feelings, it is also a record of your struggle to come to terms with the death of someone you continue to love.

III. Emotion-Focused Constructive Coping (Cont.)

<u>Cope with your anger in healthy ways</u>

Refer again to page 18 for a discussion of this important emotion. As you know, anger following a death can manifest in a variety of ways. Find constructive means of managing your anger so as not to hurt yourself or others. A related concern is forgiveness. Is there someone you've had a hard time forgiving? Who is this person? Of course you will never forget, but will there come a time in your life when you are ready to forgive? What would it take for you to forgive this person? Or does it seem impossible to do so at this point in your life?

<u>Reduce your emotional arousal</u>

1. Exercise: As noted earlier, engaging in an aerobic activity for 25 minutes or more three times a week can bring equilibrium to one's body.

2. Relaxation: Sit for five minutes as you tense and relax your body from head to toe. Use some form of yoga or meditation.

3. Prayer: For some people, quiet prayer can help to quell emotional upheaval.

INDIVIDUAL DIFFERENCES IN GRIEVING

We all grieve differently. You hear it all the time and you've read it throughout this book.

One of the types of grieving is known as *Intuitive* (feeling). The other is called *Instrumental* (thought/action). Let's see how this works.

The Intuitive—Instrumental Dimension of Grief [17]

Intuitive. Some people display their grief openly. They experience waves of emotions such as anger, guilt, sadness, and confusion. They cry. They have a great need to talk about it. These are *Intuitive Grievers*.

Instrumental. Other people tend to experience grief in thoughts and actions rather than emotional displays and more often do it alone. An Instrumental Griever may:

Work on a project	Create something new
Compose a song or write a story	Visit a place
Look at pictures or video	Engage in workaholism
Raise money for a scholarship	Think about the death continuously
Engage in sports to feel one's body	Engage in risk-taking activities

Rarely is a person totally on one side. Where are you on the scale below?

Intuitive   Instrumental
  Griever   Griever

|- -|

In general, women land more on the Intuitive side and men more on the Instrumental side. So, in reaction to a death in the family a man may see some of the women over-emoting while a woman may see the men as holding it in. Although men and women can be anywhere on the scale, our society is not typically comfortable with a man in grief who emotes too much. He may be seen as weak. By contrast, a woman who is more of an Instrumental Griever may be seen as cold. People may wonder, "What's wrong with her?"

Here are other examples of individual differences in the way people grieve:

Crying: As noted earlier, some people cry easily, others hardly cry at all.

Denial: Some people use denial as a way to get through the moment.

Hardiness: When a tragedy occurs some people seem to be highly resilient and bounce back sooner than others.

<u>Need for control:</u> When a person has a high need for control, the death of a loved one can cause a significant disruption to the view of the world.

<u>Role demands:</u> For example, some families expect one or more members to be *The Rock*—the one who holds it together while everyone else falls apart.

<u>Tendency to ask for help:</u> Some people find it difficult to reach out for help, while others do so quite easily.

<u>Religion:</u> Some people cope with grief through the comfort of religious beliefs.

<u>Cultural beliefs:</u> A person's cultural background will provide a context for one's convictions about the meaning of life, death, mourning, and afterlife beliefs.

How Do I Know When I'm Getting Better?

One of the ways to think about your grief is to look at some of the markers that indicate you are moving forward. The following are statements from bereaved people who responded to the question, *"How did you know when you were starting to get better?"*

See which ones apply to you:

I realize that it really happened and that my life has forever changed.

Sometimes a whole day has slipped by without feeling overwhelmed.

I can talk to others about the death without getting as upset.

I feel that I don't have to grieve perfectly.

It doesn't hurt as much as it used to.

I don't think of my loved one every moment and that is okay.

I want to do more with my life than "just survive."

I can laugh without feeling guilty.

The emotional roller coaster ride isn't as bad as it used to be.

I don't care as much about what other people think of me.

I feel like a light has come back on in my life—things are clearer, brighter.

Doing little things for myself is okay.

I'm not as much afraid of the future.

I'm not searching as often for that familiar face.

I begin to call or text someone and remember what I wanted to say.

I'm not as sad or depressed as I used to be.

Holidays, birthdays, and anniversaries are a little easier.

I can engage in some of the activities I had given up after the death.

The weekends aren't so long.

I can put away or give away some of the belongings and feel okay about it.

I am realizing that moving on does not mean that my love is any less.

I can experience the reminders as more positive than negative.

When another loss occurs I now understand more of the effect it has on me.

I now know both truths: I am moving on with my life, but I will never forget.

I can look back and see my progress.

I've noticed there aren't as many idiots on the freeway.

I can reach out to help other people.

I realize that I still have a lot more to do with my life.

I think less about the actual death and more about the life that was lived.

I realize that I will always carry this person in my heart and that I am a better person for having had my loved one in my life.

My Note to You

Thank you for reading this book. I hope you found validation for your feelings in these pages. By choosing to read it, you have taken an important step.

Although this book has an ending, grief seems to go on and on. There will be times in your bereavement process when things seem to be going better when—*boom*— another reminder of the devastating events surrounding the death will reactivate your emotions.

People who have read this book tell me that one of the ways they have noticed their progress is to look back over the pages and identify which reactions have changed.

In my teaching, lecturing and counseling over the years I have met literally thousands of people who were coping with grief. They have been my mentors in helping me learn and write about the bereavement process. One of the many lessons they taught me was:

While it may seem impossible at this moment, someday in the future you will look back to this time period and say, "How did I ever make it through that difficult time in my life?"

As you think about grief and joy in your life right now, if may look something like this:

Believe it or not, someday grief and joy in your life will look more like this:

Remember, there are people out there who care for you. Take life one day (or one moment) at a time and maybe someday you can be the one to offer assistance to someone else who is grieving a loss.

I wish you peace,

Bob

Acknowledgments

Thanks to those individuals who read and commented on the original version of this book. Their time and effort provided a significant contribution in the development of the first version. Thank you:

Marie Chevrier, Joe Frisino, David Sheppard, and Lynda Sheppard.

A great deal of thanks goes to the following bereaved people and professionals who provided input for the revised editions:

Fernita Bass	Phil Haldeman	de Olsen
Shawn Baugher	Teri Hansen	Ralph Olsen
Karyl Chastain Beal	Yola Hauskins	Jamie Quinlan
Ann Bekins	Amy Hausske	Tally Reynolds
Linda Coughlin Brooks	Jean Humphrey	Lynn Riegel
Betty Conley	Lori Keller	Vanessa Riley
Carol Cowherd	Carl Komor	Candace Roseberry
Ellen Curtis	Gail Lafferty	Joan Ross
Diane Dellinger	Chris Landeis	Rosemary Stolle
Don Dodson	Jeanette Landeis	Margarita Suarez
Kathi Dodson	Martha Liska	Carol Sunada
Elaine Eggebraaten	Sharon Mayer	Geri Ventura
Shelly Ellis	Rick Mirabile	Sara Weiss
Vic Ellison	Peggy Moore	Viola Williams
Linda Wong Garl	Suzn Morgan	Roman Wright
Kristal Hager	Carol Nichols	

Thanks also go to my wife, Kris, for the photo cover and book design and for her love and support all these years.

Thank you to Ron Engstrom of Desktop Publishing & Printing, Seattle, for production of this book.

A special thank you to my editor, Janée J. Baugher, MFA.

Discounts for Ordering Multiple Copies

2-10 copies:	5% Discount
11-24 copies:	10% Discount
25-49 copies:	20% Discount
50-99 copies:	30% Discount
100-499 copies:	35% Discount
500-999 copies:	40% Discount
1,000 or more copies:	50% Discount

Price: $5.00 (U.S. funds) per copy. Add $2.50 postage for a single copy. Free postage for U.S. orders of 2 or more copies.

Shipping: Canadian and out-of-U.S. orders will be billed according to postal rates.

Washington state residents add 9.5% sales tax.

Please allow 2-3 weeks for delivery.

Send Check or Money Order to:

Bob or Kris Baugher
7108 127th Pl. S.E.
Newcastle, WA 98056-1325

OR

e-mail your order and you will be billed:

b_kbaugher@yahoo.com

Other books by Dr. Baugher:

- *Understanding Guilt During Bereavement*
- *Death Turns Allie's Family Upside Down*
  with Linda Wong-Garl & Kris Baugher
- *Understanding Anger During Bereavement*
  with Carol Hankins, M.S. and Gary Hankins, Ph.D.
- *Coping with Traumatic Death: Homicide* with Lew Cox
- *After Suicide Loss: Coping with Your Grief* with Jack Jordan, Ph.D.
- *The Crying Handbook* with Darcie Sims, Ph.D.
- *In the Midst of Caregiving* with Darcie Sims, Ph.D.

Videos

- *Men and Their Grief*
- *Men and Their Grief: 20 Years Later*

REFERENCES

[1] Rubin, S.S., Nadav, O.B., Malkinson, R., Koren, D., Goffer-Shnarch, M., & Michaeli, E. (2009). The two-track model of bereavement questionnaire (TTBQ): Development and validation of a relational measure. *Death Studies, 33(4)*, 305-333.

[2] Klass, D., Silverman, P. R., & Nickman, S. L. (Eds.). (1996). *Continuing bonds: New understandings of grief.* Bristol, PA & London: Taylor & Francis.

[3] Field, N. P., Gao, B., & Paderna, L. (2005). Continuing bonds in bereavement: An attachment theory based perspective. *Death Studies*, 29, 277–299.

[4] Stroebe, M., Stroebe, W., Schut, H., Zech, E., van den Bout, J. (2002). Does disclosure of emotions facilitate recovery from bereavement? Evidence from two prospective studies. *Journal of Consulting and Clinical Psychology, 70(1)*, 169-178.

[5] Worden, J.W. (2009). *Grief counseling and grief therapy: A handbook for the mental health practitioner.* NY: Springer.

[6] Baugher, B. (2009). *Understanding guilt during bereavement.* Newcastle, WA: Caring People Press.

[7] Blank, H., Musch, J., & Pohl, R.F. (2007). Hindsight bias: On being wise after the event. *Social Cognition, 25*, 1-9.

[8] Gamino, L.A., Hogan, N.S., Sewell, K.W. (2002). Feeling the Absence: A content analysis from the Scott & White grief study. *Death Studies*, 26(10), 793-813.

[9] Stroebe, M. & Schut, H. (1999). The dual process model of bereavement: Rationale and description, *Death Studies*, 23(3), 197-224.

[10] Rando, T.A. (Ed.) (1986). *Parental loss of a child*, Champaign, IL: Research Press Company.

[11] Maas, J.B. & Robbins, R.S. (2010). *Sleep for success!* Bloomington, IN: AuthorHouse.

[12] Baugher, B. (2001). How long (according to the media) should grief last? *Columbia Journalism Review*, Mar-Apr, 58-59.

[13] Attig, T. (1996). *How we grieve: Relearning the world.* NY: Oxford University Press.

[14] Neimeyer, R. (Ed.). (2001). *Meaning reconstruction and the experience of loss.* Washington, DC: American Psychological Association.

[15] Nadeau, J.W. (1998). *Families making sense of death.* Thousand Oaks, CA: Sage.

[16] Moos, R.H. & Billings, A.G. (1982). Conceptualizing and measuring coping resources and processes. In L. Goldberger & S. Breznitz (Eds.) *Handbook of stress: Theoretical and clinical aspects.* NY: Free Press.

[17] Martin, T. & Doka, K.J. (2000). *Men don't cry...women do: Transcending gender stereotypes of grief.* Philadelphia: Brunner/Mazel.